ABSENT TONGUES

ABSENT TONGUES
BY KELWYN SOLE

*and besides you dance when you are sad
you must be from my country*
— *Tchicaya U Tam'si*

Earlier versions of these poems have been published in the following journals and on the following websites:

*Big Bridge, Botsotso, The Common,
Green Dragon, English Academy Review, LitNet,
New Contrast, New Coin, Southernrainpoetry.*

Publication © Hands-On Books 2012
Text © Kelwyn Sole 2012

First published in March 2012 by Hands-On Books

PO Box 385, Athlone, 7760, South Africa

http://www.modjaji.book.co.za
modjaji.books@gmail.com

ISBN 978-1-920397-40-1

Book and cover design: Megan Ross
Cover photograph: Liesl Jobson
Printed and bound by Mega Digital, Cape Town
Set in Arno Pro.

i.m. Jessie Amelia Anne Mary ('Annie') Sole
(née Ellis) (1912 -2006);
for Colleen, for having faith;
and for Rochelle, as always.

CONTENTS

-I-

A stammer that passes for language	11
Everyday	13

-II-

Cape of Good Hope	19
Signal Hill	21
Land	22
Tin roof	24
Nocturne	26
Not a poem on behalf of the poor	27
Small landscapes repeating birds and children	29
New country	39
Poems of the sea for me	40
Walking away	43
Outsiders	45
Chant for charming a snake	52
Breaking bread	54
The Fall	55
Real Estate	57
Breathings	59
What the sea brings	61
Voyaging	62
The letter	63
Spreading the sweetness	64
'Love is a persistent radiance' (Mills & Boon)	65
Shopaholic	67
Barefoot poem	68
Morning song (kettle out of frame)	69
I want what comes after	70

-III-

Threshold	73
A gripping story	76

I

A stammer that passes for language

    1

Driving all night ...

on my radio
just one maudlin singer
to replace another -
crackles of static -

with two
        hands steering
towards whatever
direction has
beckoned
last
    I try
        to make sense
of each augmented beat,
every concussive affectation

each time your bravado passes,
   going the other way on
      much much faster wheels

    2

- until finally

prayers and curses,
as the scalding voice
of an ambulance flares red
between the fields.

- What did you want to say to me?

3

I wanted to say

we share meaning
only as bodies in collision:

picking through strewn wreckage,
looking for a limb to recognise,

hoping to take it home.

Everyday

1

Sun under the auspice of Pisces:
entrails of a summer dragged out
so hot
      that in the market place
steam rises off the bodies of those
who wish to buy and sell themselves.
Each hour is a goat butting a fence.
A nail shrieks in my mind - factories
that torture steel nearby -

while tiny distant figures
raise parentheses of dust,
and occasionally a taxi may
guffaw to a fuller sentence.

Seasick shacks and hovels
pitch and roll
      abut the road
that falls endlessly, or rises,
across a memory of dunes.

Not far away, water
bronzes to a polluted beauty

even if nothing will make it rain.

2

From my room all I can see
are two trees, caked with dust,
arms twisted across each other
like floundering dancers,
resigning themselves
to the sun's grip.

There are ghosts that hover in the air.

They are no more the spirits of our dead
but a sadness at what might have been
had we more courage

                had we searched
further than our skins our pockets.

Though sometimes
there is expectation:
above the wizened trees,
their stubborn tap roots
sunk (I must not forget)
deep into our earth
                a margin
of clouds approaches,
and what remains of
their leaves applaud.

We wait in vain

till sunset drowns
the air we breathe
the sky we watch
with gobbets of fiery oil.

   3

The nights, oh! the nights
start off seeming different:

breezes bubble up in the darkness;
when I inch my window open
stars gibber on the quaking pane;

a distant song wavers and wavers

and it's colder. The noises of commerce
and self-congratulation stop.

Your nails squeak on the false marble
of the table as you reach out
for yet another glass,
                dodge my fingers,
tell me once again
that we're merely friends.

4

If only I could sleep.

5

My car catches splinters
of light as I chink the curtains
hoping to find it still
not stolen.
      You rustle,
turn, call out half awake
that I should come back;
keep you warm.

But I can't.

      Outside
who is it   is it also I
who quails on tiptoe,
gulps down fear, swallows
the adrenalin of need
to follow tyre-tracks
slewed inside a gate:
scrutinize this house with
only one light shining?

Don't ask me now
which one I am -
the one inside:
the one outside:

picklock, picklock.

6

Morning again, with its bray
of trucks and voices.

Each day I wonder

why I wake having dreamt
the lamentation of women,
bent over, a sound
like wasps grudging the air
or a drill making a meal
out of bone -

why again I am set off
like a waking clock.

II

Cape of Good Hope

1

Dawn's sheen off the sea mars sight   everything bent forward to cope   with wind even the mountain   squats awkwardly   a huge grey snail   feeding tirelessly from the tides   through its concrete pseudopods

the sun awakens us   coaxes a glitter from shale and sandstone   the pavements and beaches warm up   schoolchildren and crabs wriggle free   to scuttle about their business   tourists bask their bellies   as summer swells ambiguously   with seeds and rubbish

dirty morning awoken   strikes intermittent sparks from cars   dolorous processions towards town   coiling snakesure along glutted highways   our convolutions of habit

... for those going to work.

For those not going to work ...

white flesh and bald heads   pulse in shadow then light   shadow light light shadow   a relentless morse code is it worth the time to   decipher.

Ageing men linger hoping there will be someone   who will expose her breasts   though on most days   the south-easter kicks sand in their faces   and blurs vision even for us who focus   elsewhere and try at times to see a little more clearly.

Above, the sky is an ogling eye   with a cauldron for its pupil.

2

I am lounging on my backside in Solly Mowser's backyard, flicking stones with a thumb off a knuckle and there's a weedeater blustering somewhere a flyswatter proclaiming the extermination of vermin a mosquito whines above my head and someone farts

on the other side of the fence

but my eyes are only for Ateefa alongside her boyfriend Des as they trace the letters laboriously onto cardboard WE DIDN'T LIBERATE THIS COUNTRY FOR IT TO BE SOLD TO THE HIGHEST BIDDER and I try to wheedle another cig from his backpack without him seeing

but fumble it into the dirt

Teefs glances at me and there's a streak of paint a bilious green next to her lips (those uncomprehending unkissable lips) and stares hard at the crumpled paper and pen in front of me and she says, *you know Kelwyn, as kakpraat 'n siekte was is jy lankal mos begrawe...*

and I raise my middle finger in answer: *moenie jouself so jus' dra nie!*, and she's puzzled because of course she's not, we can all see she's behind this she's the thinker here she's proud of the slogan and Des likes it too, sitting right beside her, what can I say, lucky *hond*,

my memory of her unruly black curls now razored to a stubble and the presence of her wasp-sharp tongue it confuses me what can I say

confronting Red Rosa with a cellphone.

3

And for those   who will never have   the luck to work?

No one wants to speak for them   or knows how   all I can say is

in amongst this domain of enclosures   verticals intercut with horizontals   and rackrentings of stucco   townships and slums   so few can see   there are buttresses curves crooked lines   so many non-conforming angles   if you dare to look yes there are   places that maybe someone can find   new ways to crawl inside.

Hum of the quotidian. For now give us that.

Signal Hill

By the Sheikh's tomb
a kneeling teen
head thrown back
entranced by sun

forgets who he is
and doesn't see
that the blunt knife
he thought a secret

has tumbled suddenly
out of his pocket
to tremble an instant
then stir with light

Land

To be frank we're all a little bit lost
with varying degrees of certainty

now that profit   builds its newness
everywhere, insists this
is our heritage.
              Sand fills the sky
with the carious gape of summer;
the eye enflames with dust and pollen,
red sunsets, or brickgrime measling wind;
there's a flattery of drills and hammers
above the whisper of what's being
killed, the tiny dumb entreaties
of insects and plants.

                    My race,
(just like yours) has traded its outposts
- our touch - for new imaginings
of brick and glass or glass
and steel: we have
all of us become
the marauders
            we once feared,
our skins grown robust
with myths about identity
from ancestors
who instruct us still
only with their bad examples,
that subduing of women men
choose to label culture.

A bull starts to bellow, drags
its death around a tether
along with globules of dust-
flecked blood. And what's to do,
as well, with the virus of white lies
that infects us all unnoticed,
the conceit that one can own
the land?

A residue of soil
flaking piecemeal off my shoe
- are you still there, or not? -
I try to walk and find my body
is suddenly much too
heavy.

Thank God   at last
a bird starts to warble
its sweet nonsense
somewhere

beyond my vision.

Tin roof

Autumn works away like a carpenter
dismantling the promises of spring -

our shelters brought so slowly down
it's hard to recollect when each wall

fell, foretell when each corrupt plank
will crumble. Too lush a green

is the colour that warps away
from the grass to leave a yellow

dull as urine from a spiteful god,
but a reference we are used to.

To go on living, here, requires a house,
a cat, and an expectation at least

about a future where the eggs
can poach, the cat heave its body

with a thump through the small door
that human hands have sawn for it;

requires a house, preferably of stone,
squatting its grey toad weight on the land

and refusing to budge for anyone.

Such houses are no longer built.

All that remains is a sky
migrating birds fly up towards

like wrenched-out nails, a moon
that bristles with convulsions of cloud

too scrawny to bring more rain
- the dry centre of our hearts laid bare -

and stars dipping nearer to a horizon
over which they will soon loiter.

Cold batters on each face exposed
with all of its bleak hammers:

there's just no way to smile left
but to keep squinting upwards like a fool

even as our doors unhinge, eyes
turn to mirrors of broken glass.

The only way to keep warm now
is to build a dwelling out of air,

draw invisible blankets to your chin;
painstakingly think your home around you.

Mine will have already open doors,
too many rooms in case of children -

I'll call high windows into being
(to watch the sky plait a million blues)

add a family room for everyone
who may choose to be related.

I'll put a tin roof on my dreams
for any young tom with stentorian boots

that's silly enough for love. Even though
the cupboards open to only an echo

passers-by will stop amazed
that such a house can take a shape

-though never, I know, in envy.
There. Now I've no recourse but to live.

This is the house my hunger built:
the pain hides where you want it.

Nocturne

Hopeless is a word
that seeks no cover for itself –

it sits outside the blanket
of the sentence, and shivers.

Not a poem on behalf of the poor

1

The poor are lighter
than a fish-head bone:
and their words, seeming
at times guttural and heavy
in their throats as stones,
blow away on a first breeze
untroubling as dandelions.

The protocols of the rich
fatten, and promise one day
to absolve them also.
It never happens. So
they endure, dazzled
by the hope of a beauty
they think others have,
their feet at the point
of an abyss with no step,
no mirror, just knowledge
of their falling.

Snagged between horizons
and billboards
           spoken to
by those enormous beings
painted in two dimensions
with arms that terminate
in soap or handshakes
who point the way

in lieu of the tame human
parings of the State who
keep their gatherings
inside closed rooms
               - those
who perorate, or legislate,
or write on others' behalf -
in all the places where the poor
never themselves set down
their bums or thumbprints.

2

In a world of money
no one needs to recognise
the palm
not held out
because it keeps
its dignity and purpose:

and, bereft of the function
of pity they provide
for those with wealth,
the final task of the poor
is an expectation
to stay unnoticed:
to remain grateful,
to cause no trouble.

The poor, in fact,
are allowed to provide
no answers of their own:

because, if they do,
their answers finally
are to those questions
those who possess,
or squander life
on power, do not
want to hear.

Small landscapes repeating birds and children

Compass

Tourists who miss out on destinations
with less blood and fewer fantasies
will end up, slightly puzzled,
                    here

Generations

where there are those

who feel obliged
to smile each morning
in a land still full of
all that cannot be said.

The first bird
sings at precisely
five o'clock, before
fire kneads the sky.
Summer.

There are
voices of children
everywhere.

Learning

Toddlers learn
to lie even before
we menace them into
uniforms, regiment their knees
and smiles,
            teach them

old praise songs

that creak with
adages, skins, compliances:
teach them

only rumours aren't forbidden.

Listen. A young girl
sombre as an owl
in huge eyeglasses
recites her fealty
to a dead idea
from which both
her dead parents
would have shied away,
unequivocally.

History

They have vanished
from her memory:

their life's struggles
a shape trampled

as if by the weight
of a dog's pads

in frightened flight
from an angry stone.

Market forces

Stunned by sun
stunned by opulence
stunned by one's inviolable
self
    for us
the unvarying gods
of law and commerce
smile, extend
a finger
until
    they're sure they've got us
    where they want us;

then the proferred hand
closes up

into a fist

Generations

while the wind dirges between
structures of plank and iron
howls litanies for the children
of the poor
not quite out of sight

- pray to the seconds
of chance and hazard
that yours is not the child

found thrown away in secret places
without his testicles,
or with her vagina torn

but if so,
learn to mourn in secret:

whatever happens
the rich must still want to
wash up on these beaches,

clacking their pincers of money.

Grass

Fires are borne out of the wind.
The soul of the dead grass stirs,
but has nowhere to run. Stones
congratulate themselves, lulled
by an earth that forgives
only their hardness.

Green

Forest - old friend -
hide me in your somnolence.

Bird

In the fibula of a tree
soon to be broken by the wind
a *piet-my-vrou* measures out
its triplets

of descending notes
without irony, without remorse
(trickery!   what trickery!)

Blue

but the sky
is fathomless,
a blue bruise
congealing for
our pleasure.

Compass

In each sleepy ex-colonial town

the cathedral clock's
been stopped so long,
no one can now recall
quite how to tell the time

teenagers moon into
each other's eyes
in cramped pizzerias

dogs yell challenges
of posture from behind
high fences and locked gates

and, as evening creeps up
in ambush, queues
of the dispossessed
are fed once more
into the maws of taxis
till
    every
        one
           has
                vanished.

History

The wounded facade of a house
undergoing renovation struggles
through swathes of cheerful paint
to maintain an old dilapidation,
but cannot persevere -

Learning

hidden in shadows
in its garden
you bend to
your book,
and the sun
touches your cheek
as you sit
        willing
its fidelity.

Bird

Suddenly a perturbation
of doves explodes
across the sky
        but you
do not think

to look further

to where
      a falcon ghosts
its wings with threat
and breakneck beauty,
high above them.

Grass

Outside the back fence

a heavy animal
collapsing over
its forelegs

the hill's pelt thins

then, with no warning,
larks exult
out of tall, dead grass -

Green

until rain causes
other boots on the slope
to turn up divots of red

clods of earth surprised
on the far side of a wash
of green
      tipsily strewn
down the mountain

(and we still don't know
how far we, too, will slide)

Market forces

as I slip
I realise that

my pocket is no pouch
to hold herbs or trinkets
to spell away despair:
instead there's just a grinding
as the few coins gathered there
jostle against each other

then tumble out.

Blue

Small boats at the jetty
primp in their various colours,
set the teeth of the water on edge
as it's forced to mimic them,
but fails to hold them still -

History

the sea utters
condoms, splintered wood, boxes
rent from their shape, a spice sachet
(still intact) with instructions in Chinese, and
too many bottles for anyone to count

occasionally a cuttlefish or dolphin

Market forces

while, stretched away
on both sides until
they taper into distance

holiday homes in Tuscan style
flop a concrete pasta
all along the African coast.

Learning

Each day casts its vote
a new liver spot on my skin

but I hold my tongue tight
just like you, and you:

more aware every day
that in the rest of our lives

our hopes will never be fulfilled,
and we won't be elected.

Blue

The wind,
        a wraith darting
white tongues from the surf, buffets in
with gobs of bluebottles, sea-bamboo
and styrofoam abandoned
                      at my feet
after the tide

I sink into the sand,
under the relentless weight
of my body and its meandering
in the measureless boredom
of mid-afternoon.

Stone

Waves slurp away
eat up the beach

a rackety train
shakes the furniture

a mirror wobbles,
a pumice stone falls -

the room shivers
in anticipation

Learning

you raise your eyes
and look at me:
and I can feel what
you're thinking,
its traces of amazement:
the undimmed flame
trapped in your flesh -
your belly that bulges
with a future -

Bird

the day expires
          a line
of black sunbirds
          hover
attach themselves
          in turn
to orange candles
          of wild dagga
and hang briefly
          in mid air
like dark, dripping
          wax.

Generations

Clouds will sometimes
curb the sky I see.
Stars wheel, come and go.
The skin of my years
wrinkles. But I
have made my choice.

Bird

Truth shakes its feathers,
curves away in flight ...

Compass

finished for the day,
a hoarse cicada packs away
its tiny accordion:

burps one final time.

I am not so much in love with travel any longer. But the journey visits me.
— Toru Takemitsu

New country

In the soft part of our palms,
in the clasp of our own hands,
hidden between the calluses and scars,
that's where we'll find our country.

Poems of the sea for me

The sea works in my silence.
- Pablo Neruda

1

Late-rising moon:
a sprinkler, forgotten,
sighs to and fro
across the lawn

it frosts into
tiny mirrors:

elbow on the sill,
trying not to yawn,
I watch outwards

for whatever may
be there, heel
of hand crushed
into cheek.

I am so tired
of your not
being awake,
waiting

for the thin string
of dawn to tug
apart impenetrable
night -

even as
the sea in shards
of splintered light

begins to fatten
to effulgence

till land
and sea
are one

*- my fatherland's the sea,
it doesn't matter I can't swim -*

2

tomorrow will again
lure towards the shore
skeins of sun wave-dancing,
recurrent wind and spray,
the minute ships
        that steep
from smudged horizons slowly
and romantically
        to loom
and grow in bulk, solidify
into the banal carriers of goods
they really are, huckstering
along our coast.

Then, when I saunter
on the beach
I'll see

little stricken shells
void their lives
and whiten:
        feel

fleas on my legs,
sand between my teeth

... to run closer
and dive in
means to
come to

an instant's blindness,
a mordancy of salt
cold on the skin
that only shocks
until it passes, so

a swimmer
perceives differently
than before:

      I live
for this moment when
my whole world tilts;
refracts

*- my motherland
is water,
and everywhere
I step,
my feet are cold -*

   3

but as for now
I just see the sprinkler
in vain still signal
out to sea, towards
that place

from where, in turn,
no one seems on watch.

*My heartland is the ocean:
in it I'm sure to drown.*

Walking away

Those who have
never known vagrancy
plan our roads,
file reports on distances,
give us maps

are now eager to measure
the hedges and walls
behind which we hid
during the war
for a height they think
for their histories will be
appropriate.

        Once more
the blood of our past
will be recorded by scribbling
fingers across paper: measured
and made abstract
away from the places
where it spilled.

This is a nation repatched
with words so many times
we all live in its sentence

and these days no one
chooses to squint
long enough to focus
on those routes
those directions
that are neglected
that meander off everywhere,
towards the outskirts.

So embrace your sister,
shake your brother by the hand,
but make certain that you
count your fingers afterwards

- above all be careful
where you decide to walk

if no one has sanctioned
the purpose of your journey.

Outsiders

Ernesto Alfabeto Nhamuave

1

Keening is for the dead;
I'll not trouble them. Or raise
any lamentation to a past
that determines us or - worse -

construct a future by which
I think we ought to live.

So this poem is not for you
Ernesto, Mozambican, as I
watch you on television
burn and burn again, as your
likeness burns in triplicate
on paper

nor you,
Domingo Christophe,
who weeps because
you leave your child
and South African-born wife
'to flee the Makause
informal settlement
under police protection
in the wake of attacks' … .

No. This poem is for myself:

I'm my country's citizen
- content within my selfishness,
at ease when rumours pullulate -

just another lickspittle
of its languages

those bullies hunkered down
behind the tip of every tongue
arms spread wide
hands becoming fists
in protection of their children

- Hunger, Fear, Conceit, and Envy -

named for their grandparents.

2

The country
the morning newspaper
I'm reading
      claims
to mimic

      crepitates
between my fingers,
leaving me still clueless ...

a body burnt up on paper
words about bodies are just paper

I want to put down
my paper. And not be content
just to peer outside

even if the view
from my window's
breathtaking: even if
winter's early, and clouds
and still more clouds threaten
to unfurl their bells
in muttered diphthongs
of reluctant rain:

even if it's cold
- *hear that?*
      can you

I can
still hear
in my mind

the trickling down of
blood its dripping then
its coursing down

the outside
of the windows of
my private life.

3

How I wish I could say:
this is past. But I can't,
for the words
        here at the edge
of my tongue hold no future
for my country; they won't tip
over, and with relief be lost

remain a charred
blotch upon the street
where filth coagulates
tricked by dust and wind
into a multitude of disguises -

pages of a newspaper
scattered in all directions:
so quickly, there
is no sentence to read
to make sense of this.

My country -
how many name you theirs,
how many talk on your behalf!

How different that flood of words
from what it is to step *step here
I'm stepping after rain so gingerly
across an earth I love, feeling
each sole throb
in turn* ...

instead

across our line of sight
cords of silence tauten;
a string of dark stories
invisible as thread
tents flapping in high wind
guy ropes yanked out
one by one -

in midstride to be tripped up
ensnared made into
a trapped animal
trapped by this place where
I   you   they
thought we were safe ...

each strand
perhaps
a tripwire
a rope
perhaps
      our
hangman's rope.

    4

... Tents are pulled down,
folded up,
put up again -

... it is safe to go home,
the foreigners are told:

are told *what did*
he say he
said we
are sa---

- so they return to the house
which they once knew;

and then they die.

5

All of us
adrift
   swing
between anger
and regret
in the world's
hot winds

though
we're told and
once more told:

*we want each and every one
of you to be proud
of who you are -*

*your identity
your race
your country*

*(though not quite
in this way)*

the mouths
in parliament
in synagogues
churches
mosques
temples
     need us to stay true
to the ideals they have for us

the dealers in smiles

while the poor

forced to scuffle   fossick
through the rubbish bins of life
will turn bleak angry eyes on
those they think add to their burden

those who came seeking refuge

I'm poor, and no one listens
I'm poor because no one listens
I tried to find a job but
I turned on the tap for water but
what comes out
what comes out
when

under the banners
our leaders
the leaders of their people
march
only for themselves.

Authors of no destiny,
co-authors of six words:

who can I find to blame?

6

what
I want
I want my country
to pardon me
for trying to
possess it

I want to think hard
what it would be like
to be Ernesto

in a rictus of agony

to die alone
to die of cruelty
far from home
at the hands of others
at the hands of those
who should have
welcomed me here
protected me

I want to think
how his death
how each death

shames us all.

7

Enough. Where Ernesto
begged us, *stop!*
there is now
just a burnt-out stick,
a scorched half-brick,
a patch of blackening ground ... .

Even now I try
come with me
        can we
                try
to sniff the air, for a tiny instant
pure, despite the stink from the corpses
piling up besides
            all our
politicians' words?

Compatriot, friend, stranger
born with me upon this land:

- as long as we do not face
what lies here on this street,
it is our only street.

Chant for charming a snake

   1

slate-cool eyes
                 of early dawn
thick bush
woodbrush
        on the path:

                my fear
what's that rustle? is it
            there
                no
                    here?

            (in your gaze
            there is no fear)

sliding golden
          light beneath across

(a stick,
   upraised)

- what's this? -
        move,
      move
    move
       YOUR FOOT!

the stick's dropped where?

   nerveless fingers

spurt of sand

       did you see?
                           no!

the gape of
hiss of

........................it was only
........................the wind! -

the wind?

   2

..............movement
of cold flesh

a belly sliding across
........................near my hand

stirring of
slither of

eyes..wrenched open

............- what's wrong,
..............what do you fear?

- I fear wind
when it jolts light,
I fear the light
that thwarts
the wind -

..............edging through

I'm
..............lost, completely
..............lost
........................can't run through

this cloying sand...

   3

what's left?

........................to turn around:
........................and face it.

Breaking bread

By a simple madness I am
marked out by a thought of love

tucked tight into my armpit
hard and shrivelled as stale bread

secreted too deeply to be shown.

And there is no one but you.
I walk around regardless of the self

I thought I was, and my past
shucks off easily as clothes.

I am a yes without a comma

who, marked down for love,
stands here in front of you.

Hunger and solicitude: love
has no other dictionary.

And what else can my words be?

Your smile recalls my power.
Your words provoke my silence.

And all that has happened
still means to happen: your face.

My tongue's turned bread. Eat.

The Fall

Your nude leg flung out
lengthens the line
of the chair's
curve -

outside,
a declivity of lawn
evaporates into mist
- snatched glimpses of a forest -

squirrels, tiny desperate miners
with the terror of foreknowledge
clutched within their paws,

run across the grass, seek to larder
up their future in the crannies
of the earth. A wind bites,
hints at the rancour of snow:

we gaze at them through glass.

There is a coincidence of sunlight

here: with my bare skin, and the scent of you.

*   *   *

Give me your palm
before I'll even think of making love to you -
I must be sure which of your lines twists
or peters out before it should –
your union line, your mount of Saturn ...

is what you said, in your nakedness,
bending further towards the mirror,
your spine a declared rosary of bones ...

and I started thinking to myself -
as you later picked up in your slim fingers
cigarettes and keys, chased the wrinkles
from cast-off jeans by filling them
with the presence of your body, leaving
just an undertone of musk
to expire in my room -

that I want beyond all else
to enter someone who looks outside
herself constantly, looks at a world
to exceed the right omens
she thinks would augment herself -.

       *   *   *

It will not be you.

Now that you've taken the accustomed body
I thought I loved back home, through the streets,
onto the trains that multiply your distance,
through doors that use their keys as weapons,
eyes locked behind
                against sight

though I still conjure up the wen
next to your lips, the small tattoo
on your neck newly shining
                through heavy shutters
of blonde hair,

(yes, I see   all of you, nearly ...)

the thing
I can no longer bear to look at,
or to imagine,

is what is in your hands.

                    Amherst - Hove

Real Estate

Again and again
the rivets, nails, mortar,
acquiesce to the shape of a house.
A hand hit

by a hammer
heals, lives quietly within
till all loud sounds are tamed.
A fork

is dropped.
The heartrending cries of
a baby. A cellphone lullabied
to sleep.

Later, the lies
and anger of each day start
to bounce inside from wall to wall,
can be faintly

heard. Around
it all the wind politely bends,
quite heedlessly, and goes on its way,
till nothing

spills into
the street. Immobile stone.
As her consolation he will go to work.
No one senses

the frustration
that's building there, that lurks
like a man with a dull knife wearing
black at night

so no sun
can betray him. In any case,
rust is too slow and damp too sly for anyone
to fret about.

- It's really
not their fault. It's just
that love may prove less lasting than the walls
it prowls between.

Breathings

The heart is not a mirror
to show itself
to many faces

an ocean cannot be covered
like a weeping face
by your two hands

- and what is flesh to do,
in the mistakes it makes
with language?

Meaning,
there should either be no pause
or no disclosure of the words:
I love you.

* * *

I am a gypsy for love
and these words to you the horses
that carry me along, dragging
the creaking cart of my tongue.

The weight is heavy.
They stumble one by one.

Inhale mist. Exhale fire.
But if I name this thing between us
in the air, desire - what worlds would
then ignite? Mine? Yours? Must

I keep my breathing inward, wait?
When will we trust ourselves to trust?

* * *

Brazen moon: though night,
its passage, smears black across
the sky. Probes my tiny
room thereafter.

For you are all the light I
have. If I were to call out
now, no one close nearby
would hear me.

Breathe. Don't   breathe.

But night will give us
nothing, I think, that we
will not give ourselves.
Open to the fire

of the body that consumes
to toss away, we bid fair
to be consumed, then
tossed away.

Breathe.   Don't breathe.

For naked, there is
a further nakedness.
Which of us can seek
it? I need an answer,

for a promise is a word
lilting into wind. There's
no room left to dodge:
the choice is yours.

Don't breathe. Breathe. Don't -

What the sea brings

Don't trust any harbour. Already
those reflections that match each boat
turn restless, yearn to fracture:

each wave beyond the quay dishevels.

I who have no instinct for bad weather
- scudding wind, nor gale – turn
watch a late evening ditching sun

that gasps lunges out to drown

in tides of creels lost, and plastic bottles.
You contrive strong, dark fingers
through your hair. Time to head home:

beside you there's me and a nervous sea

bereft of the small white globes of gulls

now trying to outrun dark. A door shuts.
We'll pass our time in tepid rooms
that dissemble light: making dinner

then making love till we lie

in tandem, fork to spoon. Who
cannot guess which one of us
will take their sleepless turn tonight

to part the curtains, start, to see

unblinking stars begin to swarm
suddenly implacable as bees
above the black void that was sea.

Voyaging

The ship boarded. I left behind
both mooring and mountain
in dawn's washed-out light;
left cottages of pale stone
- in one you were sleeping -

saw the harbour front dwindle
touts yelling, yachts at anchor
quay at length breakwater too
all that's solid all that has stood
between me and a roistering sea.

Which of us sleeps, who stays awake?
We who knew love, to leave it, dare
we persist, face each day exposed?
Bodies tremble with longing but
briefly. Then all grows cold.

That this new light will gain force
once the breeze starts to bluster
and underfoot the deck totter
I know. At last my sight's veering
towards the sea, away from you.

From the shore love's song wavers
is further away
                in the wind's bugle
so far from those months we both
were aglow with its god. You
did not turn to me: now, turn, see

the sun's glare strike at the sea.
Over swells shear black birds:
False Bay under me. I've lost,
now I'm lost at sea. All at
sea. What cannot be fathomed

glints its last is dragged down
just another anecdote within
an archive of drowned men.
I finally see. In the long run
it's only this wind will endure.

The letter

In my garden I dropped
a letter I'd addressed to you.

Such a heavy downpour
into the eyebrows of October!
- even the trees shoved till
their hair is all shed. Time

for bedraggled old crows
to pack up their scolding, try
to drag sodden bodies to
a refuge that's dry. Like them

I'll become accustomed to this:
every road to your house
quite sopped up on a blotter
of treacherous weather. My letter

now smelling of dead snails
of mint and the brown words
dogs leave once they've passed,
all the things I had still to say...

reaching down - tips of fingers -
I knew my waist thickened
along with my heart. Then
slowly unbent. In my garden

I dropped a letter that longed only
for you.
        And left it there.

Spreading the sweetness

Thanks so much for that jar of jam.

As you guessed, it got messed on my trousers
and the plate and couch and schnauzer as well.
In the process a dab must have entered my ear
- maybe I scratched there while goggling at *Lost* -
so by the end there was nothing to do
but prod with a fingertip a trifle less icky
at the remote till the screen dimmed and blanked.

The dab - how to put this? - seems likely to stay.
Going to bed, I was ambushed abruptly
by an odour of apricots smudging the pillow
- oh, it was that easy to be lulled into sleep!
But in this new morning I've woken half-blind:
as taste smell and a dream with you in it
have coagulated bang-smack right inside one eye.

Even as it still burns, what do you think:
should I bear it for now? On your next visit
- if the eye's tearing still - it may tempt you
to a quick peck on the lid (and whom could that
harm? If done chastely, of course). Amazed at
my good taste, you'll think, *"that's really my doing?"*
then wonder, *"next time, should I try out the fig?"*

Whatever you want. But please bring more jam.

'Love is a persistent radiance' (Mills & Boon)

"intermittent power surges are likely to continue"
- Eskom

briefly glancing outwards
what do you want to
know? there are clouds.
a window creaking

   and i know
   that, right now,
   somewhere,
   to an unsuspecting child
   water offers up
   its gift of cholera

      while elsewhere
      a crowd of tyres
      strewn on the road
      blaze in front of police
      who are fast losing their
      patience at being stoned

         and still elsewhere
         there are five neighbouring
         towns on the platteland
         that've had no electricity
         nor working sewerage for
         it must be seven days now ....

- but here there's
just us pixels -

      i scratch my head
      chase flakes of thought
      they drift away like dandruff

then
   THERE! – you light up the screen again

       Hello there!
       Lo

        a teenager in a car
        red as a bum's boil
        reverses outside in
        a clash of gears and
                parks

distracted
i look back
the cursor's disappeared

      you come up again:
            Hello there!
            on broken computer …

            Love you LL I cn rite

each word flickers once, then vanishes

i would delete you
but there's nothing
to delete

      you write again

            nff said
            mst fli

        my keyboard jams

      or maybe it's just
      the letter *l*
      lllllllllllllllllllllll

        you say
        c u ina bt

the screen blackens
    i want
    dammit
    i wanted
    just to say
    love you too
        or rather
            lv u2
but

Shopaholic

Come to me at night or in the middle of the day
    there's no need to wear your shoes tight your skirts
tailored   or court the commerce of men's favours
    or be a bargain hunter instead just dance backwards
    in disrespect through the glitter of the shopping malls
    and come (to me) tonight or in the high noon of your
day I don't care   just strip off your nudity
and   come   to   me   naked

Barefoot poem

All the endless repetitions of truth,
all the mindless nibbling away
at reality: I must confess I want
to lose the ways I try

to come to words until at last
I'm tired of them. And what's to come
to me, in silence, but a woman
like you, who sitting down

on the couch will kick off her shoes
as if she's resting for merely a moment
before again departing. And then
will leave. But we both know

she, you, is here to stay:
although we'd never say it.

Morning song (kettle out of frame)

The pilgrimage of your dark eyes
discovers dawn. Now the sun
resumes its routine and draws near,
but *it* won't bring you coffee.
You lift your head, take it
from my hand as if with care
you're holding the whole world.

I want what comes after

I want what comes after:
the first lifted bucket's clang
once the rooster's all crowed out,
a keen thirst for fresh water
as sequel to that sound

your smell drying on my skin,
your fingers brushing briefly
against my stomach as you stir
awake from dozing: or, when
you've gone, an empty shape
left sprawled asleep within
the blankets on my bed.

I want what comes after:
the miraculous vigil of a moth
unburnt beside us in the sheets;
toast starting to brown, the nails
of a scabby cat across the floor,
conclaves of birds upon the eaves

the rustle of trees as they begin
to post their letters to the wind -
wind that's strong enough to blow
off a roof of morning mist, a sky
like a field that begs a plough
emerging. And the two of us
looking outside to find the dawn
to which we'll trust our bodies.

III

Threshold

1

Our world is colour
bound into matter and we
may be struck blind or deaf
the first time that we look
- that we really look - at
or listen to a colour. And not
just one but every kind, more
than we can begin to name
in our sad and broken
language.

So, if this is pretending
to be about a world
of sight and sound
and the sounds that lurk
in colours

expect something
indescribable and simple.

2

... Because today, for me,
it felt as if I was at
the beginning of the world:

as if swallows were crowding
outside
      against my window

beseeching me
to come outside,
to recognise their migrations.

So I made the obvious mistake -
I left my room.

I went out walking
from my house to yours
(do you still live there?)
across this patch of open ground

- on the way
was forced
to watch

a contrail write itself
briefly across
the page of cobalt
it made out of
a mundane blue sky,
          only
to be rubbed away -

to listen to

the chink of silence
between the breaths of
a windmill's metallic asthma
(such a decrepit, ashen sound) -

then an adder of cerise and ochre
hiss at me from out the grass -

of course,
I jumped:

these can't be
real colours!

  3

I've been told
animals dream in black & white.
I am not an animal (mostly)

and, besides, I don't
believe it.

4

So, standing here, stranded
between my house and yours
I am starting to notice
the almost-music that rises
from out the veld around me,
when I'm scarcely on the watch

for what I want to hear.
For today
        everything around me
makes me giddy

           and the earth
on which I stand seems
to make one meerkat-stretch
into the distance,
and then another,

- one step further,
and who knows

under my feet
what ground

may crumble,
then give way?

A gripping story

The frightened noon of your sentences,
as your fingers peck at the computer:
chickens that will not look up at the sky

in case it falls on their heads.
                    Words
will appear, in an urge for fantasy,
as if they were people talking,

though they are not - for they cannot
love, or sing, or shit their sickness out
onto a street, or even show you a real face

resembling your own. Despite reports
of storms hoving in from every place
to you it's all self-justifying, to you

it's still just pixels. Otherwise,
who is it you live beside, becalmed,
two bodies made of habit, whom you try

to talk into a passion? Think carefully,
for today – as every other day –
you hold a small world in your hands.

Quotations from the following sources are acknowledged:

Pablo Neruda *The Poetry of Pablo Neruda*
(New York, Farrar, Straus & Giroux, 2005);

Toru Takemitsu *Confronting Silence: Selected Writings*
(London: Scarecrow, 1995);

Tchicaya U Tam'si *Selected Poems*
(London: Heinemann, 1970).

Other titles by hands-on books

Lava Lamp Poems
by Colleen Higgs

Difficult to Explain
edited by Finuala Dowling

A Lioness at my Heels
by Robin Winckel-Mellish

Looking for Trouble
by Colleen Higgs

www.ingramcontent.com/pod-product-compliance
Lightning Source LLC
Chambersburg PA
CBHW010047090426
42735CB00020B/3414